CW01513296

"This vocabulary k
based on a true story."

-Albert B. Squid

SQUARE ROOT OF SQUID PUBLISHING

PREFACE

Who wants to study boring vocabulary words?
Nobody!!! That's who. But what if learning new words
was fun and easy? That's exactly what this book,
"Big & Fancy Words That Might Make You Smarter..er
(+ really long subtitle here), is for. This book is
designed for you to learn only one word in one day.
So instead of trying to remember a list of words
at the same time, with only one big & fancy word a
day you can really let that word sink into your
brain, remember the definition throughout the day,
you can use that word in real conversations you
have that day, and see and hear that word used
in books, movies, or when eavesdropping on people.
This book contains one word a day for 366 days of
the year (that's right, leap year is included too),
that you can learn every day or skip days. Each
page is dated, so depending on which date you turn
to in the book, that's the word of that day. Each
page comes with the word of the day, its type, its
meaning, a funny example sentence, and synonyms
and antonyms. Throw this book on the back of the
toilet, in your car, on the coffee table, or next to
your bed, in your underwear drawer, in your
private jet, in the shed, or wherever you do daily
things. Build your vocabulary, study for the SATs,
or gain skills for word games and crossword
puzzles, but do it slow and easy and possibly with a
chuckle here or there.

-Albert B. Squid

(adjective)

impecunious

Having little or no money.

I am used to my impecunious lifestyle, surviving on whatever I can find in the dumpster behind the restaurant.

poor, poverty-stricken, broke

rich, well-to-do, affluent

(adjective)

FALLACIOUS

MEANING

To be false. Incorrect.

EXAMPLE

Saying the earth is flat is a fallacious statement.

SIMILAR

wrong, false, misleading

OPPOSITE

right, correct, truth

PUGNACIOUS (adjective)

MEANING

Ready to fight and argue.

EXAMPLE

Although the dog was small he had a pugnacious character.

SIMILAR

aggressive, scrappy, warlike

OPPOSITE

calm, quiet, relaxed

UMBRAGE (noun)

A feeling of being offended.

MEANING

EXAMPLE

The girl took umbrage with the teacher for not using her preferred pronoun "them".

SIMILAR

anger, discomfort, offense

OPPOSITE

delight, happiness, pleasure

(noun)

VICISSITUDE

The ups and downs,
the highs and lows of
something. MEANING

EXAMPLE

The vicissitudes of life turned
the man into a raging alcoholic.

SIMILAR

challenge, change, ordeal

OPPOSITE

stability, sameness, placid

(adjective)

DIDACTIC

Intended to teach a lesson.   MEANING

EXAMPLE

The man was accused of mansplaining when he gave the woman a didactic speech on how to drive a car.

SIMILAR

educational, informative

OPPOSITE

misleading, uninstructive

(noun)

ICONOCLAST

A person who doesn't follow rules and attacks popular beliefs. MEANING

EXAMPLE

If you take a knee while the national anthem is playing, you might be considered an iconoclast.

SIMILAR

deviant, free spirit, maverick

OPPOSITE

conformer, supporter

(noun)
SOLIPSISM

The thought that you are the most important person in the world. *MEANING*

EXAMPLE

Tom has become so arrogant about how much money he has, it's now bordering on solipsism.

SIMILAR

self-centered, narcissism

OPPOSITE

selflessness, generosity

(noun)

neopHYTe

A new person to a new activity.

MEANING

EXAMPLE

The seniors were sick of all the neophytes on campus.

SIMILAR

novice, beginner, newcomer

OPPOSITE

veteran, pro, expert

BEGUILE (verb)

To entice with tricks.

MEANING

EXAMPLE

The actor was so good at his craft, that he was able to beguile the audience into thinking he really was a cat.

SIMILAR

deceive, mislead, charm

OPPOSITE

repel, be honest with

(verb)
OBFUSCATE

To make unclear. To confuse.

MEANING

EXAMPLE

The murderer used words that were meant to obfuscate the truth of where the body was.

SIMILAR

blur, perplex, obscure

OPPOSITE

clarify, clear up, reveal

(adjective)

DOGMATIC

Strongly believing *MEANING* something to be true.

EXAMPLE

His dogmatic views on the Bible really made the atheist angry.

SIMILAR

authoritative, opinionated

OPPOSITE

open-minded, accepting

(noun)

ABERRATION

Something that's MEANING
different than normal.

EXAMPLE

The thought that vampires
exist, is a complete aberration.

SIMILAR

abnormality, deviation

OPPOSITE

normality, sameness, delusion

(adjective)

mendacious

MEANING

To be **dishonest**.

EXAMPLE

Amber broke up with Will because of the mendacious story he told her of where the money came from.

SIMILAR

deceitful, false, insincere

OPPOSITE

truthful, honest, sincere

RECALCITRANT

MEANING

1. Having a bad attitude toward authority. (adjective)

2. A rebel. (noun)

EXAMPLE

The recalcitrant punk rockers defaced the mayor's picture with dog poop.

SIMILAR

rebellious, defiant, unruly

OPPOSITE

passive, agreeable, manageable

(adjective)

LICENTIOUS

MEANING

Sexually immoral.

EXAMPLE

Lauren ended up getting herpes because of her licentious behavior.

SIMILAR

fast and loose, promiscuous

OPPOSITE

moral, pure, virginal

(adjective) COGENT

MEANING

Very convincing.

EXAMPLE

The cult leader's cogent speech led to the followers drinking the poisoned juice.

SIMILAR

logical, compelling, powerful

OPPOSITE

unimportant, weak, ineffective

(adjective)

SURREPTITIOUS

MEANING

Done secretly.

EXAMPLE

The man had a surreptitious desire to wear women's clothes.

SIMILAR

private, secret, stealthy

OPPOSITE

open, public, in plain sight

RESCIND (verb)

MEANING

To officially cancel.

EXAMPLE

Greg decided to rescind his petition calling for all residents to be allowed to keep exotic pets.

SIMILAR

overturn, revoke, reverse

OPPOSITE

enforce, create, enact

(adjective)

ONEROUS

MEANING

Being troublesome.

EXAMPLE

She decided to take on the onerous task of cleaning out the overloaded litter box.

SIMILAR

difficult, a burdon, hard

OPPOSITE

light, soft, easy

BILK

(verb)

To cheat out of something.

MEANING

EXAMPLE

The sneaky lawyer bilked his clients out of millions of dollars.

SIMILAR

swindle, cheat, trick

OPPOSITE

enrich, be generous to

(adjective)
FORTUITOUS

MEANING

Happening by chance.

EXAMPLE

It was a fortuitous accident that landed him the job as vice president of the company.

SIMILAR

unexpected, fortunate

OPPOSITE

predictable, planned

ZEPHYR

(noun)

MEANING

A gentle breeze.

EXAMPLE

When she farted, it was like a zephyr in the forest, soft and gentle.

SIMILAR

slight wind, small gust

OPPOSITE

furious wind, hurricane

(noun)

PULCHRITUDE

MEANING

Physical beauty.

EXAMPLE

She lost her last ounce of pulchritude the minute her false teeth fell out.

SIMILAR

hotness, attractiveness

OPPOSITE

ugliness, grossness

(adjective)

GARRULOUS

Very talkative about
stupid things. MEANING

EXAMPLE

After just three beers, his
conversation became a garrulous
lecture on the importance of
nose hair.

SIMILAR

gabby, motormouthed

OPPOSITE

quiet, reserved

(adjective)

OBDURATE

Determined not to change.

MEANING

EXAMPLE

Jane remained obdurate on the topic of the vaccine.

SIMILAR

stubborn, not flexible

OPPOSITE

changeable, wishy-washy

(adjective)

EGREGIOUS

Really bad in an obvious way. MEANING

EXAMPLE

The actor spoke his lines in such an egregious accent that the audience believed it to be bordering on racism.

SIMILAR

gross, blatant, terrible

OPPOSITE

great, likable, adorable

(adjective)

GREGARIOUS

Fond of hanging around with people.   MEANING

EXAMPLE

Rich's gregarious nature always made him the life of the party.

SIMILAR

Sociable, fun, cordial

OPPOSITE

introverted, unfriendly

(noun)
modicum

MEANING

A small amount.

EXAMPLE

Rachael's outfit is so 2008, proving she doesn't have even a modicum of taste.

SIMILAR

speck, scrap, fragment

OPPOSITE

big amount, heap, a ton

(adjective) **BEREFT**

MEANING

Lacking something.

EXAMPLE

His face was bereft of color after she scared the crap out of him.

SIMILAR

cut off from, robbed of, upset

OPPOSITE

satisfied, full, content

enervate (verb)

To make something weak.

MEANING

EXAMPLE

The only way to enervate his grip was to tickle him.

SIMILAR

to wear out, to tire, to exhaust

OPPOSITE

to energize, to invigorate

(verb)
ARROGATE

MEANING

To take without permission.

EXAMPLE

The boy was trying to arrogate all the cookies leaving the other kids with crumbs.

SIMILAR

seize, acquire, secure

OPPOSITE

give, offer, refuse

(adjective)
INIMICAL

Tending to be harmful.

Even though she is an inimical chick, I still think she is hot.

hurtful, destructive

nice, respectful, friendly

(noun) # PAUCITY

A small amount of something. MEANING

EXAMPLE

There is a paucity of information surrounding the Metaverse.

SIMILAR shortage, rareness,

OPPOSITE abundance, a lot of

(adjective)

SWARTHY

MEANING

Dark-skinned.

EXAMPLE

Being at sea for so long, gave the pirate a swarthy complexion.

SIMILAR

tanned, dusky, tinted

OPPOSITE

fair, pale, lack of color

(adjective)

VITRIOLIC

MEANING

Harsh and/or bitter in tone or substance.

EXAMPLE

The teacher's vitriolic critique of the girl's art project brought her to tears.

SIMILAR

mean, cruel, tart, nasty

OPPOSITE

nice, kind, pleasing

LARGESSE (noun)

Generosity in giving things to others. MEANING

EXAMPLE

The rapper showed his largesse by making it rain twenty dollar bills on the strippers.

SIMILAR

charity, kindness, self-sacrifice

OPPOSITE

miserliness, selfishness

PITHY

(adjective)

Brief but powerful. Usually with words. MEANING

EXAMPLE

"Be yourself: everyone else is already taken." is a pithy saying by Oscar Wilde.

SIMILAR

forceful, full of vigor, concise

OPPOSITE

wordy, lengthy, weak

(noun) # CUPIDITY

Greed for money and objects.

It was the thief's cupidity that made him go back for the second diamond even though it was risky.

materialism, money hungry

generosity, a giving nature

(verb)

EXACERBATE

MEANING

To make worse.

EXAMPLE

Trying to pull his tongue off the frozen pipe would only exacerbate the problem.

SIMILAR

intensify, aggravate, worsen

OPPOSITE

reduce, make better

(adjective)
ANTEDILUVIAN

MEANING

Made a long time ago.

EXAMPLE

Brad didn't like his father's antediluvian taste in music.

SIMILAR

ancient, prehistoric, old-fashioned

OPPOSITE

new, relevant, modern

COBBLER

(noun)

MEANING

A person who makes and repairs shoes.

EXAMPLE

I would rather have my shoes repaired by a cobbler than buy a new pair.

SIMILAR

shoemaker, shoe repair person

OPPOSITE

not a shoemaker

(noun)

TURPITUDE

MEANING

Acts of wickedness.

EXAMPLE

For her acts of turpitude toward the other girls, the cheerleader was asked to leave the squad.

SIMILAR

immorality, corruption, evil

OPPOSITE

honor, virtue, kindness

ARCANE (adjective)

Known to only a few people. MEANING

EXAMPLE

NFT's are an arcane premise to my parents.

SIMILAR

secret, mysterious, hidden

OPPOSITE

open, in plain sight

(adjective)

AMOROUS

Inclined toward sexual
desire and love.

MEANING

EXAMPLE

The amorous couple turned
their bedroom into a love den
complete with furry handcuffs.

SIMILAR

erotic, passionate, lustful

OPPOSITE

unloving, cold, hateful

(noun)

PLENITUDE

MEANING

Having a lot of something.

EXAMPLE

The party was rocking, with great music and a plenitude of adult beverages.

SIMILAR

abundance of, large quantity

OPPOSITE

lack of, scarcity of, need for

(adjective)

ECLECTIC

MEANING

Having a style that is a mixture of many things.

EXAMPLE

The design of Frank's house was very eclectic with corrugated metal sheets and chainlink fence over traditional wood siding.

SIMILAR

broad, wide-ranging, diverse

OPPOSITE

common, specific, similar

(adjective)

ANACHRONISTIC

Belonging to the wrong time period. MEANING

EXAMPLE

The boy's profile pic of Abraham Lincoln with a mohawk and earring seemed a bit anachronistic.

SIMILAR

out-of-date, ancient, dated

OPPOSITE

fresh, new, modern

(verb) CONSTRUE

MEANING

To analyze the meaning of something.

EXAMPLE

Getting an "F" in English class shouldn't be construed as an act of punishment by your teacher.

SIMILAR

interpret, understand, decode

OPPOSITE

confuse, obscure

(noun)
INTERLOCUTOR

A person who takes part in a dialogue or conversation. MEANING

EXAMPLE

I asked Rose to join as another interlocutor to our discussion on zombies.

SIMILAR

speaker, talker, interviewer

OPPOSITE

introvert, quiet person

PROBITY

(noun)

MEANING

The quality of being honest.

EXAMPLE

Jackson showed a great deal of probity when he told the principal it was him who gave Jimmy the wedgie.

SIMILAR

decency, honor, virtue

OPPOSITE

badness, deceitfulness

CAROUSE (verb)

MEANING

To get wasted and have a good time with friends.

EXAMPLE

Sara loved to carouse on Saturday nights, but hated the hangovers the next day.

SIMILAR

binge-drink, frolic, whoop it up

OPPOSITE

to be a party-pooper

(noun)
ABNEGATION

The act of rejecting something.

EXAMPLE

The boy's abnegation to vegetables led to his problem with obesity.

SIMILAR

rejection, refusal, surrender

OPPOSITE

acceptance, approval, agreement

(noun)

PLETHORA

A large amount of something.

EXAMPLE

There's a plethora of information about transgender marriage in India on the internet.

SIMILAR

excess amount, surplus

OPPOSITE

a small amount, a little bit

(noun)

DEMAGOGUE

A person who preys on the passions of people to get their way. MEANING

EXAMPLE

Hitler will go down in history as the biggest demagogue of all time.

SIMILAR

instigator, rabble-rouser

OPPOSITE

peacemaker, pacifist

(adjective)

emoLLienT

MEANING

Soothing to the skin.

EXAMPLE

The emollient cream helped relieve the burning sensation on my butt from the poison ivy.

SIMILAR

moisturizing, softening, relieving

OPPOSITE

harsh, rough, burning

PLAUDIT (noun)

MEANING

An expression of praise.

EXAMPLE

The band entered the arena to the plaudits of the crowd.

SIMILAR

applause, cheer, congratulations

OPPOSITE

criticism, sneer, condemnation

PRESAGE

(verb) To give a warning.

(noun) A warning.

Does the rapid advancement of artificial intelligence presage the future that we are doomed as a species?

foreshadow, foretell, warn

to keep secret, hide

inAne

(adjective)

To be **stupid**.

Thinking the earth is flat is such an inane belief that people who believe that should be slapped.

dumb, uneducated, foolish

smart, intelligent, sensible

FEB 29

(adjective)

BISSEXTILE

Having an extra day as in leap year. MEANING

Leo was born on a EXAMPLE bissextile-year, so even though he looked 20 years old, he was actually 5 years old.

SIMILAR

today, February 29, leap-year

OPPOSITE

March 1st, not February 29

(adjective)

PRODIGIOUS

Impressively great in extent, size, or degree.

It would have been such a prodigious opportunity to study the art of hand shadows with Master Greg.

tremendous, amazing, fantastic

crappy, unexceptional

(verb)

MASTICATE

MEANING

To chew.

EXAMPLE

The actor forgot to turn off his microphone, so the sound of him masticating could be heard by the whole crew.

SIMILAR

munch, chomp, crunch

OPPOSITE

decompress, stay idle

(verb)

CAPITULATE

MEANING

To surrender.

EXAMPLE

The mother capitulated to her son's request for another piece of cake, even though he had five already.

SIMILAR

back down, give in, submit

OPPOSITE hold out, resist

(adjective)

eBULLieNT

Very energetic in a positive way. MEANING

EXAMPLE

My uncle is usually shy and introverted, but after a couple of beers he becomes an ebullient party animal.

SIMILAR

cheerful, bubbly, high-spirited

OPPOSITE

depressed, gloomy

(noun)
OXYMORON

A contradictory group of words.

MEANING

EXAMPLE

"Pretty Ugly" and "Jumbo Shrimp" are examples of oxymorons.

SIMILAR

paradox, contradiction

OPPOSITE

sameness, not contrary to

IMPUTE (verb)

To say that someone or something has done something wrong. MEANING

EXAMPLE

Her neighbor tried to impute that the dog took a poop on his lawn.

SIMILAR

attribute, blame for

OPPOSITE

forgive, absolve, approve

(noun)
ANTITHESIS

MEANING

The exact opposite.

EXAMPLE

David is a such a brat, the utter antithesis of his well mannered sister.

SIMILAR

reverse, inverse, flip side

harmony, sameness OPPOSITE

(adjective) # DOUR

Very serious or harsh.

MEANING

EXAMPLE

The usual dour face of Mr. Bradford turned cheerful when Mrs. Bradford wore that mini skirt.

SIMILAR

unfriendly, gloomy, dismal

OPPOSITE

cheerful, happy, smiling

(adjective)
exIGenT

Needing urgent action.

MEANING

EXAMPLE

The frostbitten toe had to be cut off due to exigent circumstances.

SIMILAR

pressing, demanding

OPPOSITE

not important, insignificant

(adjective)

PROTEAN

MEANING

Able to change easily.

EXAMPLE

The alien is a protean being, able to turn into anything it sees in an instant.

SIMILAR

shifting, chameleonlike

OPPOSITE

constant, consistent

(adjective)

EPISTOLARY

In the form of written letters.

MEANING

EXAMPLE

The couple's long-distance epistolary relationship ended when the man got arthritis.

SIMILAR

written messages, love letters

OPPOSITE spoken, conversed

(noun)
GOURMAND

A person who enjoys eating and drinking too much.

Stan was quite the gourmand, so much so, that his pants have to be custom-made to fit him.

glutton, pig, chowhound

picky-eater, fussy

(verb)
INURE

To make someone or something used to hardship.

MEANING

EXAMPLE

Ted became inured to the smell of human waste after a year of working for the septic tank company.

SIMILAR

harden, toughen, acclimatize

OPPOSITE sensitize, soften

(adjective)

DIAPHANOUS

MEANING

Very thin and translucent.

EXAMPLE

The obese man's butt crack could be seen through his swimsuit made of diaphanous material.

SIMILAR

sheer, lightweight, delicate

OPPOSITE

thick, opaque

VAPID (adjective)

MEANING

Have a lack of creativity.

EXAMPLE

While listening to the girl's vapid story about shoe shopping, I could barely keep my eyes open.

SIMILAR

boring, dull, lifeless, bland

OPPOSITE

creative, interesting, full

DIRGE

(noun)

A song or poem for the dead.

MEANING

EXAMPLE

A dirge played on the boombox as we flushed our pet goldfish down the toilet.

SIMILAR

requiem, dead march

OPPOSITE

celebration song for life

(adjective)

INEBRIATED

To be drunk.

MEANING

EXAMPLE

Danny was so inebriated on St. Paddy's Day that he threw up in his Irish cap.

SIMILAR

wasted, sloshed, plastered

OPPOSITE

sober, cognizant, alert

(noun)

CRAPULENCE

Sickness after drinking too much alcohol. MEANING

EXAMPLE

From the sound of dry heaving coming from the bathroom, you could tell Danny was a victim of crapulence.

SIMILAR

hangover, nausea, illness

OPPOSITE

fit, healthy, feeling great

(noun)
ACCOUCHEMENT

MEANING

The process of giving birth.

EXAMPLE

After his wife's accouchement, because no scissors could be found, he had to cut the umbilical cord with his teeth.

SIMILAR

childbirth, delivery, labor

OPPOSITE not giving birth

DESPOT

(noun)

A cruel dictator.

MEANING

EXAMPLE

Jenny called her father a despot after he grounded her and took her phone away.

SIMILAR tyrant, oppressor

OPPOSITE democrat, liberal

(noun)
INVECTIVE

Insulting and abusive language. MEANING

EXAMPLE

The invective coming from the gangster's mouth made Benny run for his life.

SIMILAR

swears, curses, bad language

OPPOSITE

praise, kind language

(adjective)

MAUDLIN

MEANING

Tearfully sentimental.

EXAMPLE

After three martinis, Janis's expression turned maudlin as she dialed her ex-boyfriend's number.

SIMILAR

emotional, weepy, self-pityingly

OPPOSITE

upbeat, cheerful, confident

(adjective)

PENURIOUS

Very poor.

EXAMPLE

The now penurious rapper was once living large, but he eventually blew all his money on cars and jewelry.

SIMILAR

poverty-stricken, lacking money

OPPOSITE

rich, prosperous, loaded

(adjective)
SANGUINE

Cheerfully optimistic and hopeful. MEANING

EXAMPLE

Jordan was in a sanguine mood even though his house was on fire.

SIMILAR

bullish, confident, positive

OPPOSITE

negative, unhappy, hateful

(adjective)
TACITURN

MEANING

Speaking very little.

EXAMPLE

Although Sheila is usually a taciturn woman, get a few drinks in her and look out.

SIMILAR

quiet, silent, introverted

OPPOSITE

boisterous, loud, talkative

(adjective)

PERNICIOUS

Very harmful.

EXAMPLE

The comedian was "canceled" due to his pernicious sense of humor.

SIMILAR

deadly, hurtful, wicked

OPPOSITE

favorable, good, divine

(adjective)

ABSTRUSE

MEANING

Difficult to understand.

EXAMPLE

Kim finds English to be one of the most abstruse languages he has ever studied aside from Arabic.

SIMILAR

puzzling, complex, complicated

OPPOSITE

obvious, concise, clear

INNATE (adjective)

Existing in someone from birth. MEANING

EXAMPLE

The boy had an innate talent to bend his finger completely back until it touched the back of his hand.

SIMILAR

hereditary, inborn, built-in

OPPOSITE

received, acquired, given

DENIGRATE (verb)

To **say bad things** about a person or a thing. MEANING

EXAMPLE

Peter tried to **denigrate** my reputation by telling the cool kids I crapped my pant once on the school bus.

SIMILAR

bad-mouth, attack, slander

OPPOSITE

praise, celebrate

(adjective)

ePHeMeRAL

MEANING

Lasting a short time.

EXAMPLE

Wearing parachute pants, mesh shirts, and one leather glove, was an ephemeral fashion trend of the '80s.

SIMILAR

short-lived, brief, temporary

OPPOSITE

permanent, long term

(verb)

VITUPERATE

To insult with harsh language.

My wife would vituperate me on a daily basis because I would leave little bits of toothpaste in the sink after brushing, so I'm single now ladies.

attack, scold, abuse

praise, honor,

(noun)
MACHINATION

MEANING

A crafty trick or scheme.

EXAMPLE

Some of his April Fools Day machinations have gone terribly wrong in the past.

SIMILAR

plans, ploys, plots, trickery

OPPOSITE

truthfulness, honesty

(noun)
ANATHEMA

Something or someone that one really hates. MEANING

EXAMPLE

The view that men and women share a bathroom may seem anathema, but in the end, we are all just humans.

SIMILAR

monstrosity, pariah, wrong

OPPOSITE

friend, prize, correct

(adjective)

FATUOUS

Not smart.

Cindy realized she made a fatuous choice to marry Ted when she found out that Ted liked collecting roadkill.

stupid, childish, silly

intelligent, witty, creative

EXPIATE

(verb)

MEANING

To make up for something that one did that was bad.

EXAMPLE

To expiate for cheating on her boyfriend, she gave him permission to do the same.

SIMILAR

make good again, fix

OPPOSITE

blame, damage, mess up

(adjective)

PUERILE

MEANING

Immature and silly.

EXAMPLE

Putting fake poop on the teacher's chair is such a puerile act of disrespect.

SIMILAR

childish, juvenile, babyish

OPPOSITE

mature, grown-up, sensible

(adjective)
AMBIVALENT

Not sure about someone or something. MEANING

EXAMPLE

When it comes to wearing stripes or plaids, I am ambivalent, so I wear both at the same time.

SIMILAR

doubtful, unsure, confused

OPPOSITE

certain, clear

(adjective)

TRUCULENT

Quick to argue.

EXAMPLE

Don't ever say "figure skating isn't a sport for men" in front of Bradley, he becomes truculent and will slap you.

SIMILAR

confrontational, argumentitive

OPPOSITE

friendly, cooperative, kind

(adjective)

UBIQUITOUS

Being everywhere at the same time.

MEANING

EXAMPLE

The ubiquitous drunken men dressed as Santa plagued the streets on Christmas Eve.

SIMILAR

all-over, popular, wide-reaching

OPPOSITE

limited, not present, scarce

(noun)

PARTURITION

MEANING

The act of giving birth.

EXAMPLE

The father was not allowed in the room during the parturition but could hear the sweet sound of his newly born daughter from the waiting room.

SIMILAR

delivery, labor, childbirth

OPPOSITE

incubation, pre-natal

(adjective)
execRaBLe

MEANING

Very bad or unpleasant.

EXAMPLE

The sight of the boy pulling out a big booger and eating it was so execrable to the woman that she almost puked.

SIMILAR

awful, terrible, digusting

OPPOSITE

pleasant, good, desirable

(adjective)
ASSIDUOUS

Showing great care.

MEANING

EXAMPLE

Writing a book is a very assiduous process that takes a lot of perseverance and a lot of coffee.

SIMILAR

diligent, careful, painstaking

OPPOSITE

lazy, slothlike, non-productive

(adjective)

CONVIVIAL

The quality of being friendly and enjoyable.

MEANING

At first, the party's atmosphere was chill and convivial but soon turned into a rager when that jam came on.

EXAMPLE

SIMILAR

Sociable, agreeable, pleasant

OPPOSITE

unfriendly, unpleasant

(verb)

DISCOMFIT

To make someone MEANING embarrassed or uneasy.

EXAMPLE

The cashier discomfited Ryan in front of everyone when she said "If you can't pay for everything, maybe put some items back!".

SIMILAR
to rattle, to upset

OPPOSITE
reassure, make comfortable

(noun)
LEGERDEMAIN

The skillful use of one's hands like in a magic trick.

Was it the magician's great skill of legerdemain that made the man's wallet disappear, or was it really magic?

sleight of hand, trickery

openness, honesty

(adjective) **TORPID**

To be inactive or slow moving. MEANING

EXAMPLE

After eating five cheeseburgers and a mini pizza, his body was in a torpid state.

SIMILAR

sluggish, fatigued, lifeless

OPPOSITE

energized, full of life, active

ONOMATOPOEIA (noun)

Words that describe sounds.

MEANING

EXAMPLE

"Splash", "Boom", and "Bang" are examples of onomatopoeia.

SIMILAR

sound descriptions

OPPOSITE

words not describing sounds.

TOADY (noun)

A person who praises someone in order to get something. MEANING

EXAMPLE

The student became the teacher's toady by bringing her an apple every day.

SIMILAR

butt-kisser, brown nose

OPPOSITE

a sincere person, honest

connive (verb)

MEANING

To plan secretly.

EXAMPLE

It's so crazy that Randal would connive against his grandmother to make her change her will.

SIMILAR

plot, scheme, conspire

OPPOSITE

tell the truth, be honest

(noun) # DUPLICITY

MEANING

The act of saying different things to different people.

EXAMPLE

The mean girls would always use the strategy of duplicity when talking about the new students to make them feel unwelcome.

SIMILAR

deception, shenanigans

OPPOSITE

honesty, integrity, honor

(noun)

CIRCUMLOCUTION

Using too many words in order to confuse. MEANING

The dictator's use of EXAMPLE circumlocution was a way of leading his people to believe they should pay higher taxes.

SIMILAR

beating around the bush

OPPOSITE

to the point, clear, concise

(adjective)

INCHOATE

MEANING

Not fully formed.

EXAMPLE

Although Brad loved styling hair, the idea of becoming a professional hairstylist was still an inchoate idea in his head.

SIMILAR

immature, unshaped, unformed

OPPOSITE

complete, grown, full-blown

(adjective)

PHLEGMATIC

MEANING

Not easily excited.

EXAMPLE

After 25 years of marriage, John remained phlegmatic when his wife dropped her robe revealing a tight one-piece bathing suit.

SIMILAR calm, cool, poised

OPPOSITE

excitable, quick-tempered

(verb) ABSCOND

MEANING

To leave secretly.

EXAMPLE

That witch stole my heart and then absconded with my best friend and all my money.

SIMILAR

to flee, escape, run away

OPPOSITE

to stay, arrive, remain

(noun)

GUMPTION

The qualities of confidence and courage. MEANING

EXAMPLE

It takes a lot of gumption to tell your boss his breath smells like a mixture of fried chicken and baby diapers.

SIMILAR

nerve, backbone, initiative

OPPOSITE

weakness, lacking confidence

(adjective)

DISPARATE

Different in every way.

The two brother's preferences for innie or outie bellybuttons were so disparate they resorted to spitting at each other when they talked about it.

contrasting, diverse, various

sameness, similar, unique

(adjective)
PALPABLE

MEANING

Able to be touched or felt.

EXAMPLE

The tension in the air was palpable when a fight broke out between Jim and Amber about the toilet seat being left up.

SIMILAR

distinct, noticeable, recognizable

OPPOSITE unseen, unfelt

(adjective)
INSIDIOUS

Gradually spreading in a harmful way.   MEANING

EXAMPLE

Pam's insidious gossip about Lauren broke her down and eventually lead her to quit band camp.

SIMILAR

subtle, sneaky, dishonest

OPPOSITE
straight-forward, honest

PEJORATIVE

MEANING

(adjective)
Expressing disapproval.

(noun)
Word meaning disapproval.

EXAMPLE

After the postman kicked the turkey, he continued to yell at it in a pejorative manner.

SIMILAR

abusive, insulting

OPPOSITE

complimentary, praising

QUIXOTIC (adjective)

MEANING

Unrealistic ideals.

EXAMPLE

Even though Grant knew being a professional figure skater was a quixotic idea, he wanted to pursue it anyway.

SIMILAR

impossible, useless, starry-eyed

OPPOSITE

practical, sensible

(noun) ALACRITY

Willing and ready.

The boy loved the smell of manure and his alacrity showed as he dove headfirst into the pile of horse poop.

eagerness, enthusiasm, zeal

laziness, reluctance

(verb)

enGenDeR

MEANING

To bring about something.

EXAMPLE

When Jacob got a wedgie from Thad in the locker room, it engendered feelings of embarrassment in front of his friend.

SIMILAR

cause, generate, bring forth

OPPOSITE

repress, stop, prevent

(noun)

COMPUNCTION

Feeling of guilt one gets when one does something wrong. MEANING

EXAMPLE

Hunter had no compunction when he took the last slice of pizza even though his girlfriend hadn't had any yet.

SIMILAR

worries, anxiousness, regret

OPPOSITE

happiness, no remorse

eXTOL (verb)

MEANING

To praise highly.

EXAMPLE

My mother would always extol the virtues of cleanliness, but I grew up to be a slob.

SIMILAR

rave about, congratulate

OPPOSITE

criticize, make fun of

DURESS (noun)

The use of force on someone to get them to do what you want. MEANING

EXAMPLE

Under duress, the man would give his whole paycheck to his wife and receive a small allowance.

SIMILAR

pressure, intimidation, threats

OPPOSITE

free will, help, comfort

(noun)

SUBJUGATION

The use of force on someone to get them to do what you want. **MEANING**

EXAMPLE

The subjugation of the Mexican people by Nepoleon could be tolerated no longer, so the people fought back.

SIMILAR

conquer, overthrow, suppress

OPPOSITE

freed, liberated, let go

(adjective)
INVETERATE

Having a habit that's hard to quit. MEANING

EXAMPLE

Gary was such an inveterate gambler that he lost everything he had including the family cow.

SIMILAR

deep-rooted, ingrained

OPPOSITE
temporary, fleeting

(noun)

PROCLIVITY

A natural tendency to like something.

MEANING

EXAMPLE

He had a proclivity for the finer things in life, however, he also had only thirty-five dollars to his name.

SIMILAR

preference, fondness, liking

OPPOSITE

distaste, disliking

(noun)
QUANDARY

A state of confusion as to what to do. MEANING

EXAMPLE

Heather was in a quandary as to whether she should get a Brazillian butt lift or a new nose.

SIMILAR

predicament, dilemma, trouble

OPPOSITE

solution, success

CAVORT

(verb)

MEANING

To dance or jump around.

EXAMPLE

During the party, Greg and Tina continued to cavort while standing on tables and wearing lampshades on their heads.

SIMILAR

frolic, play, leap, have fun

OPPOSITE

lounge, hover, loiter

Acumen (noun)

Ability to make good judgments in one particular thing. MEANING

EXAMPLE

Running a pub not only takes a strong liver but also a lot of business acumen.

SIMILAR

sharpness, cleverness, flair

OPPOSITE

ignorance, inability

(adjective)

MALODOROUS

MEANING

Smelling badly.

EXAMPLE

The malodorous breath coming from Sean's mouth brought back memories of the smell when a donkey coughed on me.

SIMILAR

stinky, rank, foul-smelling

OPPOSITE

fragrant, good-smelling

ABJECT (adjective)

MEANING

The condition of being extremely bad.

EXAMPLE

His toenails were so long they put everyone that saw them in an abject state of nausea.

SIMILAR

worthless, low, terrible

OPPOSITE glorious, grand, great

MAY 13

(noun)

TRISKAIDEKAPHOBIA

The fear of the number 13.

MEANING

Triskaidekaphobia was so widespread throughout the Architecture community, Architects designed buildings without a 13th floor.

EXAMPLE

SIMILAR

superstition with the number 13

OPPOSITE

no fear of the number 13

PARIAH (noun)

MEANING

A person who is outcast from a social group.

EXAMPLE

Leo became a pariah of the art world when he peed in a urinal that was actually a very expensive piece of art.

SIMILAR

reject, unwanted person

OPPOSITE

popular, socialite, cool

(adjective)
SOLICITOUS

MEANING

Full of concern.

EXAMPLE

There was a solicitous look on his face as he gently pulled the candy bar out of the hands of the obese child.

SIMILAR

worried, attentive, caring

OPPOSITE

aloof, heartless, unfeeling

(adjective)

APOCRYPHAL

Being of doubtful creditability.

The apocryphal story of the kid who died from eating pop rock candy and cola is known by many who grew up in the '80s.

fictitious, untrue, made-up

true, honorable

(adjective)

eXTRANeous

To be not relative to a matter.

MEANING

EXAMPLE

The instructor's speech on the anatomy of a chicken was so full of extraneous information that it put me to sleep.

SIMILAR

beside the point, pointless

OPPOSITE

meaningful, helpful

INCUMBENT

(adjective) Holding a set of responsibilities.

(noun) Someone who holds an office.

MEANING

EXAMPLE

1. It was incumbent upon him to get me the rash cream.

2. The incumbent president was an idiot.

SIMILAR

required, binding, essential

OPPOSITE
optional, flexible

(adjective)

CONTENTIOUS

Likely to cause an argument. MEANING

EXAMPLE

Ellen has some really contentious views when it comes to putting pineapple on pizza.

SIMILAR

debatable, controversial

OPPOSITE
not controversial

(adjective)

MAWKISH

To be so sappy it's
sickening.

MEANING

EXAMPLE

Martin's mawkish apology was so
fake that I threw up in my
mouth.

SIMILAR

overemotional, cheezy

OPPOSITE

cool, hip, slick

(adjective)

HETEROGENEOUS

Being made up of different parts.

MEANING

EXAMPLE

The United States is an example of a heterogeneous society in which many ethnicities live in one country.

SIMILAR

assorted, mixed, diverse

OPPOSITE

homogeneous, sameness

(adjective)

Homogeneous

Being made up of the same parts.   MEANING

EXAMPLE

North Korea is an example of a homogeneous society in which one race lives in one country.

SIMILAR

oneness, sameness

OPPOSITE

heterogeneous, mixed

(adjective)

PELLUCID

MEANING

1. To be very clear, see-through.
2. Easily understood.

EXAMPLE

My once pellucid swimming pool is now a murky shade of green thanks to the first-grade pool party we had.

SIMILAR

transparent, crystal-clear

OPPOSITE

cloudy, murky, unclear

(adjective)

STAID

To be quite serious and proper. MEANING

EXAMPLE

The British dude, once known for his staid behavior, now parties every night with his harem of girlfriends.

SIMILAR

traditional, unadventurous

OPPOSITE

fun-seeking, daring

(noun)
ACCRETION

MEANING

A gradual build-up.

EXAMPLE

The accretion of crime in our city is due to our idiot mayor firing half the police force.

SIMILAR

gross, increase, gain

OPPOSITE

decrease, loss, dispersion

(noun)

CONGRUITY

The state of things fitting together nicely. MEANING

EXAMPLE

Even though the couple fought daily, there was a congruity to their marriage that was undeniable.

SIMILAR

harmonization, compatibility

OPPOSITE

unevenness, not regular

(adjective)

eQUIVOCAL

Having two or more possible meanings. MEANING

EXAMPLE

The equivocal theme of the NFT left the buyer wondering if he bought a masterpiece or a piece of dog poop.

SIMILAR

ambiguous, not sure, unclear

OPPOSITE

guaranteed, exact

(noun)

PLATITUDE

MEANING

Something that is said so often it becomes boring.

EXAMPLE

The girl was sick and tired of hearing the platitudes about how a student should dress always spewing from her mother's mouth.

SIMILAR

commonplace, cliche', ya ya ya

OPPOSITE

interesting, exciting, fun

onus

(noun)

A burden.

The onus of having to babysit her younger brother every Friday night led Zoe to the habit of screaming into her pillow.

responsibility, obligation, duty

benefit, advantage

(adjective)

REDOUBTABLE

Very strong in character.

MEANING

EXAMPLE

Even though Mark is short and goofy looking, it turns out he is a redoubtable fighter with a strong uppercut.

SIMILAR

fearsome, invincible, mighty

OPPOSITE

weak in character, frail

(verb)

ABROGATE

1. To cancel something.
2. To not do something.

MEANING

EXAMPLE

In the world of shady school politics, Cecil was willing to abrogate his position as class president for the small sum of 12 dollars and 50 cents.

SIMILAR

repeal, overturn, remove

OPPOSITE

to add, to fulfill, institute

CIRCUMVENT (verb)

MEANING

To avoid by going around.

EXAMPLE

After the dog emptied the trash on the floor, it was able to circumvent punishment by giving its owner a big wet smooch.

SIMILAR

evade, by-pass, get away with

OPPOSITE

get caught, go straight into

(verb)

expunge

MEANING

To get rid of something.

EXAMPLE

Tom's name was expunged from a list of possible suspects in the stolen underwear case when it was made clear that Tom doesn't ever wear underwear.

SIMILAR

erase, delete, remove

OPPOSITE

continue, accept, maintain

(adjective)

FRACTIOUS

Easily upset.

My father has always been a fractious man but when he got upset my mother could calm him down by tickling his feet.

grumpy, bad-tempered, grouchy

friendly, agreeable, happy

(adjective)
MACABRE

Having a gruesome atmosphere connected to death. MEANING

EXAMPLE

Her sense of humor is quite macabre seeing how her jokes always have something to do with death.

SIMILAR

horrifying, shocking, terrifying

OPPOSITE
pleasant, upbeat, fun

ABJURE (verb)

> To reject a belief.
>
> MEANING

EXAMPLE

He had to abjure his religion because he got caught eating a banana on a Thursday which was not allowed.

SIMILAR

give up, renounce, abandon

OPPOSITE

claim, accept, approve

CANDOR
(noun)

The quality of being honest.

Had it not been for Cindy's candor, John would not have put on deodorant and would still stink to this day.

truthfulness, frankness

insincerity, indirectness

extant (adjective)

MEANING

Still existing.

EXAMPLE

The extant can of mystery meat in his fridge has a very odd color and smell.

SIMILAR

alive, undestroyed, remaining

OPPOSITE

dead, extinct, nonexistant

JOVIAL (adjective)

To be upbeat and friendly.

MEANING

EXAMPLE

Getting a mani-pedi always puts Gloria in a jovial mood.

SIMILAR

happy, cheerful, jolly

OPPOSITE

gloomy, hateful, negative

(adjective)

IDIOSYNCRATIC

Being unique to a certain person. MEANING

EXAMPLE

William was well known for his idiosyncratic diet of bugs fried in butter.

SIMILAR

individual, personal, distictive

OPPOSITE

common, usual, sameness

PROMULGATE (verb)

MEANING

To announce publicly.

EXAMPLE

The CEO is trying to promulgate his company's product "Wetties" as the best elderly diaper out there.

SIMILAR

broadcast, spread, promote

OPPOSITE

keep secret, keep hidden

(adjective) # STOLID

Showing little emotion.

EXAMPLE

Toby had a stolid look on his face when his parents informed him his hamster, Scrappy, had just passed away.

SIMILAR

calm, chill, unemotional

OPPOSITE

hyper, wild, lively, emotional

TIRADE (noun)

MEANING

A long angry speech.

EXAMPLE

My jerk boss went into a tirade because I cut my toenails next to the salad bar.

SIMILAR

criticism, rant, loss of temper

OPPOSITE

peace, chill, calm, cool, collected

WILY (adjective)

MEANING

To be crafty and sly.

EXAMPLE

The coyote used some very impressive and wily maneuvers when trying to catch that bird for his dinner but to no avail.

SIMILAR

devious, cunning, tricky

OPPOSITE

stupid, unprepared, naive

ACCEDE
(verb)

1. Agree to a demand.
2. To take a position or office.   MEANING

EXAMPLE

Larry acceded to his wife's nagging and finally took the trash out.

SIMILAR

accept, give in to, allow

OPPOSITE
deny, refuse

(adjective)

VOCIFEROUS

MEANING

To be **very loud** and forceful when talking.

EXAMPLE

The coach was met by some very vociferous parents who demanded that he make it mandatory for all players to wear jockstraps regardless of gender.

SIMILAR

vocal, vigorous, insistant

OPPOSITE

quiet, demure, silent

JUNE 16

(adjective)
BOMBASTIC

Someone or something trying to be bigger than they/it actually are. MEANING

EXAMPLE

The rapper's lyrics are so bombastic that one would think he was loaded when in fact he still lives in his mom's basement.

SIMILAR

stuck-up, boisterous, pompous

OPPOSITE

humble, straightforward

(verb)

RELEGATE

To put someone or something in a lower position or rank. MEANING

EXAMPLE

The soldier was relegated to latrine duty after accidentally running over the general's foot with a tank.

SIMILAR

downgrade, demote, lower

OPPOSITE

upgrade, promote, higher

(noun)

CORPULENCE

MEANING

The condition of being fat.

EXAMPLE

Because of the boy's extreme corpulence, it was impossible to find him a seesaw partner.

SIMILAR

obese, overweight, tubby

OPPOSITE

slim, fit, in shape

(adjective)

UTILITARIAN

Made to be useful.

EXAMPLE

The architect created a very utilitarian design for the factory looking like a big black box with no window.

SIMILAR

efficient, practical, functional

OPPOSITE

dysfunctional, decorative

(adjective)

VISCERAL

Coming from a feeling and not from intellect.

The voice actor had such a deep and sensual voice that it had a visceral effect on the women who heard it.

emotional, deep down, reactive

intellectual, logical

(adjective)

DIDACTIC

Intended to teach something.

MEANING

EXAMPLE

The father gave his son a rather didactic lecture on why it's not civilized to pick one's nose in public.

SIMILAR

informative, educational

OPPOSITE

uninstructive, uninformative

UPBRAID (verb)

To scold someone.

MEANING

EXAMPLE

The child was upbraided for touching the soft spot on the baby's head when he knew that it could cause brain damage.

SIMILAR

criticize, yell at, chew out

OPPOSITE

congratulate, celebrate

(verb) # evince

MEANING

To make something clear.

EXAMPLE

He tried to evince the fact to his colleagues that dressing like a ballerina was perfectly within his rights according to the company's handbook.

SIMILAR

reveal, show, exhibit, display

OPPOSITE hide, cover up

(adjective)
TANGENTIAL

Having an indirect MEANING connection to something.

EXAMPLE

The road map is filled with tangential projects that the NFT can be used in rather than the main project, which is the game.

SIMILAR unrelated, peripheral

OPPOSITE

central, on the mark

(verb)

AGGRANDIZE

MEANING

To increase something.

EXAMPLE

Chelsea's attempt to aggrandize her stature as a cool kid failed when the student body found out she plays Dungeons and Dragons.

SIMILAR

multiply, enlarge, broaden

OPPOSITE

decrease, make small

INTRANSIGENT

(adjective) Not willing to agree.

(noun) Someone who refused to agree.

MEANING

EXAMPLE

Because of Heather's intransigent personality, we were unable to come to an agreement that Mexican food is better with cilantro.

SIMILAR

stubborn, uncompromising

OPPOSITE

willing, flexible

(adjective)

LACONIC

Using few words to express meaning.

After Jane was fired for shopping for clothes online at work she made a laconic speech about her need to look good for clients.

short and sweet, brief

long-winded, chatty

(adjective)

PUNCTILIOUS

Extremely attentive to detail. MEANING

EXAMPLE

He was so punctilious when it came to plucking his nose hairs, other people started asking him to pluck theirs as well.

SIMILAR

picky, diligent, meticulous

OPPOSITE
careless, absent-minded

SERENDIPITY (noun)

The occurrence of finding something by chance.

MEANING

EXAMPLE

It was pure serendipity when Steven met his future wife at a cock fight run by the Russian mob.

SIMILAR

luck, coincidence, fluke

OPPOSITE

unlucky, zemblanity

(noun)

ZEMBLANITY

The occurrence of finding something by intent.

MEANING

EXAMPLE

It was pure zemblanity when Ellen met her future husband at a cock fight run by the Russian mob.

SIMILAR

unlucky, serendipity

OPPOSITE

luck, coincidence, fluke

(adjective)
eTHEREAL

Being very light and airy.

The sounds coming from his guitar were so strange and ethereal that you would think he was an alien.

fragile, delicate, soft

heavy, chunky, imposing

(adjective)

AMENABLE

Willing to do anything and easily controlled. MEANING

EXAMPLE

When Maria was pregnant her husband was so amenable to her wishes that he would make her a cheeseburger with peanut butter at 3 in the morning.

SIMILAR

moldable, submissive, flexible

OPPOSITE

stearn, uncooperative

VILIFY

(verb)

To say or write something bad about someone or something. MEANING

EXAMPLE

The newspaper tried to vilify the superhero, calling him a mere vigilante, but the people didn't buy it for a second.

SIMILAR

insult, criticize, attact

OPPOSITE

honor, respect, comment

AUTARKY (noun)

MEANING

Economic independence.

EXAMPLE

There are some voters out there that think our country would prosper if it were to run under a policy of autarky.

SIMILAR

freedom, self-sufficiency

OPPOSITE

dependant, needy

(noun) BANE

Something that causes trouble or harm. MEANING

EXAMPLE

This ingrown toenail has become the bane of my existence.

SIMILAR

destruction, torture, torment

OPPOSITE

comfort, pleasure, relief

EDICT (noun)

An official order given by an authority.

MEANING

EXAMPLE

Dad laid down the edict that we couldn't have a party while he was away, but it was mostly ignored.

SIMILAR

command, rule, mandate

OPPOSITE

request, proposal

(adjective)
GRATUITOUS

1. Not necessary and
unwanted. MEANING
2. Given away free.

EXAMPLE

The movie was filled with gratuitous scenes of monkeys scratching their butts.

SIMILAR

needless, unjustified, unpaid

OPPOSITE

necessary, needed, costly

(adjective)

OBSTREPEROUS

MEANING

Uncontrollable and loud.

EXAMPLE

The birthday party became obstreperous once the donkey and the car full of clowns showed up.

SIMILAR

rowdy, disruptive, unruly

OPPOSITE

restained, quiet, calm

(adjective)
PERTINACIOUS

Strongly determined and opinionated.

MEANING

EXAMPLE

My grandma is so pertinacious when it comes to winning at shuffleboard that she will bite her opponents right before they shoot.

SIMILAR

relentless, persistent

OPPOSITE

holding back, flexible

SCURRILOUS (adjective)

To be offensive toward someone to ruin a reputation. MEANING

EXAMPLE

Mike's scurrilous lies about me being born with two butt cracks made me the laughing stock of the office.

SIMILAR

insulting, abusive, slanderous

OPPOSITE

polite, decent, moral

(noun)
APPROBATION

Approval or praise for someone or something.

Christine was looking for approbation from her husband for the meatless meatloaf and cream corn dinner she made for him.

appreciation, support

criticism, disapproval

(noun) # DEARTH

MEANING

A shortage of something.

EXAMPLE

The janitor complained about the dearth of quality urinal puck products on the market these days.

SIMILAR

lack, scarcity, deficiency

OPPOSITE

abundance, full, plethora

(noun)
OSTRACISM

A method of exclusion from a group. MEANING

EXAMPLE

Tony risked ostracism from his team for refusing to shower after the game.

SIMILAR

rejection, blacklisting, snubbing

OPPOSITE

welcoming, acceptance, take in

(noun)

HOOSEGOW

A slang word for prison.

EXAMPLE

The French dude was thrown in the hoosegow for protesting the use of the words french fries, french toast, and french dressing.

SIMILAR

jail, slammer, the big house

OPPOSITE

outside, anywhere but jail

(noun)
DISREPUTE

MEANING

The state of not being respected by people.

EXAMPLE

Frank's reputation had fallen into disrepute after he started his "beans only" diet and would always fart in church.

SIMILAR

dishonor, shame, humiliation

OPPOSITE

respect, honor, glory, pride

eXHORT (verb)

To strongly urge.

MEANING

EXAMPLE

Al was exhorted by his neighbor to keep his dog from pooing on his lawn or there would be consequences.

SIMILAR

encourage, pressure, push

OPPOSITE

discourage, ignore, leave alone

(adjective)

TRENCHANT

MEANING

To be sharp in expression.

EXAMPLE

The scientist's trenchant criticism of the flat-earther's theories made me laugh so hard a little poop came out.

SIMILAR

piercing, keen, vigorous

OPPOSITE

vague, unclear

PENCHANT (noun)

A strong liking for doing something. MEANING

EXAMPLE

John had a penchant for searching for rocks that looked like famous people.

SIMILAR

passion, fondness, enjoyment

OPPOSITE

hatred, loathing

CALUMNY
(noun)

A false statement made to ruin ones reputation.

MEANING

EXAMPLE

Mr. Thomas was a victim of calumny when his client accused him of double-dipping his nachos in salsa.

SIMILAR

bad-mouthing, slander

OPPOSITE

truth-telling, approval

PONTIFICATE (verb)

To make pompous statements. MEANING

EXAMPLE

Megan loves to pontificate about her knowledge of the didgeridoo and several other aboriginal instruments.

SIMILAR

being a know-it-all, to preach

OPPOSITE

be modest, be humble

(adjective)

SPURIOUS

Seeming to be real but is not.

MEANING

EXAMPLE

Although it looked pretty good, everyone knew Bert was bald under that spurious wig.

SIMILAR

fake, false, make-believe

OPPOSITE

genuine, real, authentic

(adjective) # TRITE

To be boring from too much use.

MEANING

EXAMPLE

He tried to be cool by using the expression "straight up", but I found it trite and so 1987.

SIMILAR

overused, stereotyped, stale

OPPOSITE

fresh, new, original

(noun)
BLANDISHMENT

Nice words used in order
to get something.

MEANING

EXAMPLE

Telling Grace that she is hot was
the blandishment Stan used in
order to get her to buy his old
piece of crap car.

SIMILAR

flattery, smooth talk, coaxing

OPPOSITE

criticism, ridicule, insult

DEBAUCHERY (noun)

Behavior that is excessive.

MEANING

EXAMPLE

After a night of debauchery, Helen could not find her shoes, her car, or her boyfriend.

SIMILAR

craziness, wickedness

OPPOSITE

pure, uncorrupt, clean

(noun)

MAELSTROM

1. A powerful water whirlpool. MEANING
2. A violent situation.

EXAMPLE

After eating all that cheese it would take a maelstrom to flush down what Jack deposited in the toilet.

SIMILAR

vortex, turbulence, chaos

OPPOSITE

order, calm, harmoney

(adjective)
neFARIOUS

MEANING

To be wicked.

EXAMPLE

The vegetarian governor's nefarious plan to ban the sales of hot dogs in the state backfired when he realized they were delicious.

SIMILAR

evil, monstrous, atrocious

OPPOSITE

nice, pleasant, holy

(adjective)
OFFICIOUS

MEANING

Being too eager to help when it is unneccessary.

EXAMPLE

I was upset when Dr. Skidmore used an officious tone with me saying I should quit eating bacon with every meal.

SIMILAR

self-assertive, bossy, pushy

OPPOSITE

laid back, chill, aloof

munIFICenT (adjective)

MEANING

Being very generous.

EXAMPLE

The billionaire made munificent donations to the Holy Alien Watermelon Church until it was revealed that the church was, in fact, a cult.

SIMILAR

big-hearted, charitable, giving

OPPOSITE

miserly, cheap, frugal

(noun)
VERACITY

The quality of always being truthful. MEANING

EXAMPLE

At first, I doubted the veracity of Leonard's statement that pigs could fly, but now I'm not so sure.

SIMILAR

honesty, correctness, sincerity

OPPOSITE

falseness, incorrectness

(adjective)

DISINGENUOUS

MEANING

Being slightly dishonest.

EXAMPLE

Clark was being disingenuous when he said the mole on my forehead with hair growing out of it made me look even more beautiful.

SIMILAR

dishonest, two-faced, sneaky

OPPOSITE

ingenuous, honest, frank

(adverb)

OSTENSIBLY

Looking like something, but not really. MEANING

Mark was ostensibly EXAMPLE withdrawing money for groceries but it turns out he needed it to buy yarn for his addictive knitting habit.

SIMILAR

seemingly, apparently

OPPOSITE

truly, really, genuinely

(verb)

espouse

1. To commit to.
2. To get married.

EXAMPLE

Those that espouse the idea that it's okay to cook fish in the office microwave should be fired.

SIMILAR

welcome, accept, support

OPPOSITE

oppose, shun, reject

(noun)

VESTIGE

A small piece of something that is disappearing or no longer exists.   MEANING

EXAMPLE

There is not a vestige of truth in the rumor that Bill liked to wear women's underwear under his mechanic's uniform.

SIMILAR

relic, imprint, a remainder

OPPOSITE

wholeness, total

(adjective)
noisome

MEANING

Having a really bad smell.

EXAMPLE

The dog decided to poop right in front of the fan filling the room with cool, yet noisome air.

SIMILAR

nasty, unpleasant, stinky

OPPOSITE

pleasant, agreeable

(noun)

PARADIGM

A pattern or model of something. MEANING

EXAMPLE

Putting pants on two legs at a time goes against the paradigm of the correct way to put pants on.

SIMILAR

prototype, example, standard

OPPOSITE

change, diversion

(adjective)

INEXORABLE

MEANING

Impossible to stop.

EXAMPLE

The inexorable fighting between his parents led Jimmy to live in the treehouse for the rest of his senior year.

SIMILAR

nonstop, relentless, persistant

OPPOSITE

preventable, stoppable

(adjective)

eRUDITe

Showing or having great knowledge gained through study. MEANING

EXAMPLE

The erudite professor could speak for hours about poetry but was an idiot when it came to computers.

SIMILAR

well-read, academic, scholarly

OPPOSITE

ignorant, uneducated

(verb)
BLOVIATE

To speak or write in a stuck-up way. MEANING

EXAMPLE

I feel that you just bloviated verbal diarrhea on me and now I need to shower.

SIMILAR

declare, lecture, ramble

OPPOSITE

to be quite, silent

(verb)

eschew

MEANING

To avoid something.

EXAMPLE

To be a good Christian you should eschew the teachings of the Church of Satan.

SIMILAR

renounce, steer clear of

OPPOSITE

indulge in, join, jump in

(adjective)
WINSOME

Charming in a simple way.

With his hands, face, and clothes covered in manure, a winsome smile suddenly appeared on Willy's face.

sweet, attractive, lovable

gloomy, glum, sour, ugly

NADIR (noun)

The lowest point of a situation. MEANING

EXAMPLE

The nadir of my career came when I was caught sleeping in the supply closet while hugging a mop.

SIMILAR

darkest hour, rock bottom

OPPOSITE

climax, peak, pinnacle

(adjective)

AMORPHOUS

MEANING

To be shapeless.

EXAMPLE

Rita has an amorphous personality, one minute she gives me a cupcake, and the next minute she smashes it in my face.

SIMILAR

unshaped, undefined, vague

OPPOSITE

definite, shaped

(adjective)
GRANDILOQUENT

Stuck up in language, manner, and style.

MEANING

EXAMPLE

That British dude tried using a grandiloquent way of speaking to make me look like a moron in front of my girlfriend.

SIMILAR

pompous, arrogant

OPPOSITE

unpretentious, concise

(adjective)

IMPETUOUS

MEANING

Impulsive behavior without thought of the outcome.

EXAMPLE

The impetuous thief thought he stole a random white car, but it turns out it was the mob boss's car.

SIMILAR

reckless, unplanned, rushed

OPPOSITE

cautious, careful, considered

(adjective)
SANCTIMONIOUS

Acting morally better than someone else. MEANING

EXAMPLE

The pastor continued to be sanctimonious even after he got drunk on wine and drove the tractor naked.

SIMILAR

holier-than-thou, smug

OPPOSITE

humble, honest

PALLIATE (verb)

MEANING

To relieve pain.

EXAMPLE

The laughing gas helped to palliate Chris's tooth pain but it also made him think that he was the supreme leader from the planet Zefron.

SIMILAR

ease, soothe, lessen

OPPOSITE

aggravate, worsen

(adjective)

APATHETIC

Showing no interest or concern. MEANING

EXAMPLE

My grandpa remained apathetic to the cause of me trying to scare the crap out of grandma with an air horn.

SIMILAR

emotionless, uninterested

OPPOSITE

caring, passionate, eager

(adjective)

MULTIFARIOUS

Having many different pieces.

MEANING

Daniel's life was full of EXAMPLE multifarious activities such as taxidermy, painting rocks, and squirrel mud wrestling.

SIMILAR

diverse, numerous, multiple

OPPOSITE

single, uniform, one

(noun)
INTIMATION

The action of making known with hints. MEANING

EXAMPLE

They had no intimation that the car would not start because there was a banana stuck in the tailpipe.

SIMILAR

suggestion, indication, signal

OPPOSITE

disregard, ignoring

(verb) # eLICIT

To draw out information or a reaction. MEANING

EXAMPLE

The cop tried to elicit information from the man about the whereabouts of the missing cheesecake.

SIMILAR

extract, bring forth, trigger

OPPOSITE

discourage, oppose, restrict

(noun)
PREDILECTION

A particular liking for
something. MEANING

EXAMPLE

Her predilection for guys with
no eyebrows and who own a
camel is lucky for me because I
have those credentials.

SIMILAR

fondness, soft spot, affinity

OPPOSITE

dislike, hatred

(noun)
EQUANIMITY

MEANING

The state of being calm while under pressure.

EXAMPLE

Fiona maintained her equanimity while standing in the middle of the mosh pit.

SIMILAR

coolness, self-control, poise

OPPOSITE

anxiety, stress, agitation

(noun)
ZEITGEIST

The feeling or spirit of a particular time.   MEANING

EXAMPLE

The best two words to describe the zeitgeist of the '80s are "heavy" and "metal".

SIMILAR

feeling, flavor, mood, trend

OPPOSITE

ancient, bygone, antique

(noun)

SYCOPHANT

A person who flatters to get what they want.

MEANING

EXAMPLE

The actress was a well-known sycophant around Hollywood always telling the big wigs what they wanted to hear.

SIMILAR

brown-nose, suck up, flatterer

OPPOSITE

slacker, loafer

PICAYUNE

(adjective)
Referring to things small and worthless. MEANING
A small cheap coin.(noun)

EXAMPLE

Fifty-five dollars is a picayune amount to pay for a vacation to Mexico, although you will have to get there riding a donkey painted like a zebra.

SIMILAR petty, minuscule, tiny

OPPOSITE

big, huge, expensive

(noun)
DICHOTOMY

MEANING

The division of two things that are totally different.

EXAMPLE

There is a dichotomy between people who like having their backs waxed and those that do not.

SIMILAR

separation, split, contrast

OPPOSITE

harmony, oneness, sameness

(noun)
euPHemism

A nicer word used in the place of a harsh word.

EXAMPLE

"Backed up worst than the Hover Dam" is a funny euphemism for being constipated.

SIMILAR

substitute, replacement

OPPOSITE

to the point, a blunt word

(adjective)

SUPERCILIOUS

The state of being arrogant. MEANING

EXAMPLE

When I asked the waiter if they serve shrimp, he said "we serve everyone equally sir!" in a supercilious voice.

SIMILAR

pompous, snobby, stuck up

OPPOSITE

humble, modest, unpretentious

(adjective)

VICARIOUS

MEANING

Having experiences through other people.

EXAMPLE

Because Dennis is bald, he gets a vicarious thrill watching the lifeguard run his fingers through his thick curly hair.

SIMILAR

secondhand, indirect, derived

OPPOSITE

direct, personal

(noun)
HEDONIST

A person who only seeks pleasure. MEANING

EXAMPLE

Being the ultimate hedonist, Burt eats caviar every day and bathes only in goat milk imported from Madagascar.

SIMILAR
thrill seeker, pleasure seeker

OPPOSITE
hermit, monk, loner

ERSATZ (adjective)

MEANING

Being an inferior substitute.

EXAMPLE

My basement is covered with ersatz wood paneling and on top of that are many hair-band posters and souvenir concert tickets.

SIMILAR

artificial, imitation, fake

OPPOSITE

real, genuine, original

(adjective)

PRECOCIOUS

To be advanced in development. MEANING

EXAMPLE

The engineer's son was such a precocious child that he had coded his first video game at the age of six.

SIMILAR

mature, advanced, gifted

OPPOSITE

slow, dull, moronic

(noun)

ACRIMONY

MEANING

Anger and bitterness.

EXAMPLE

The old man's acrimony comes out when the neighborhood kids steal his lawn gnomes.

SIMILAR

nastiness, harshness

OPPOSITE

good-will, softness

(adjective)
PEEVISH

MEANING

Easily annoyed.

EXAMPLE

Having little sleep, the mother became peevish as she changed yet another diaper while her husband just drank beer on the couch.

SIMILAR

crabby, irritable, grumpy

OPPOSITE

easy-going, flexible

(adjective)

UNTENABLE

Not able to be defended.

MEANING

EXAMPLE

We almost got away with it but it soon became an untenable situation once Lori spilled the beans about spilling the beans on the sofa.

SIMILAR

invalid, unarguable, absurd

OPPOSITE

defendable, strong, sturdy

(adjective)

PERFUNCTORY

Done fast without attention to detail.

The perfunctory design of the new line of t-shirts lacked creativity and also had no hole to put your head or arms through.

hasty, careless, quick

careful, detailed

(noun)

misnomeR

The wrong name or title of something. MEANING

EXAMPLE

Calling the lazy dog "Fast Freddie" is a misnomer when in fact the dog only eats, sleeps, and poops.

SIMILAR

misnamed, miscalled,

OPPOSITE

correct name

(noun)
CACOPHONY

An annoying mix of loud sounds.   MEANING

EXAMPLE

The cacophony of voices coming from the group of girls was so ear-piercing, that I felt that my eardrums would pop and leak ear juice on my salad.

SIMILAR

racket, caterwauling

OPPOSITE

quiet, peace, silence

(adjective)
MACHIAVELLIAN

MEANING

To be cunning.

EXAMPLE

Vinny went over his Machiavellian plan to con the housewives out of their money by dressing like a famous singer and selling them low-quality vacuum cleaners.

SIMILAR

devious, tricky, sneaky

OPPOSITE

trustworthy, straightforward

SCINTILLATING (adjective)

MEANING

1. Shimmering brightly.
2. Showing skillfulness.

EXAMPLE

After **25** years of marriage, scintillating moments are very rare, except for that one time on Labor Day when we kissed on the veranda.

SIMILAR

exciting, shinning, glimmering

OPPOSITE

matte, dull

(adjective)

VERBOSE

Containing or using more words than needed.

MEANING

EXAMPLE

Zachary's verbose explanation of how fruit flies mate made me so tired, that I fell asleep, fell off my chair, and cracked my front tooth.

SIMILAR

wordy, talkative, rambling

OPPOSITE

to the point, direct, concise

(adjective)

unrequited

Not given back or felt in return.

MEANING

EXAMPLE

Sara loved her hamster "spanky" so much, but it was unrequited love for spanky would ignore her and leave his droppings in her sock drawer.

SIMILAR

one-sided, disregarded

OPPOSITE

reciprocated, given back

(verb) FINAGLE

To use tricks to get what you want. MEANING

EXAMPLE

Jess finagled her way into college by offering fresh fish to the head of admissions every day.

SIMILAR

swindle, deceive, cheat

OPPOSITE

ignore, decline, refuse

(adjective)
TENACIOUS

Keeping a strong hold on
something.   MEANING

EXAMPLE

The Awkward Nerds team used
a tenacious defense to beat
the Jovial Jocks on their home
turf.

SIMILAR

clinging, tight, immovable

OPPOSITE
weak, loose

(adjective)

CAPRICIOUS

Likely to **suddenly** change.

MEANING

EXAMPLE

Jeff has such a capricious personality in that one minute he tells you that you are pretty and the next minute that you are a **swamp donkey**.

SIMILAR

unstable, impulsive, wild

OPPOSITE

consistent, stable

(adjective)

enIGMATIC

Being difficult to understand.

Nancy sent me a very enigmatic text, it said "cow-tipping and dumpster diving with wine and snacks, my place.".

puzzling, mysterious, weird

normal, straightforward

ABASH

(verb)

To make someone feel uncomfortable or embarrassed. MEANING

EXAMPLE

Kevin tried to abash me by saying I had poop on my jeans in front of Jody, but he was wrong, it was just chocolate pudding.

SIMILAR

ruffle, fluster, upset, disturb

OPPOSITE

encourage, reassure

DECAMP
(verb)

To quickly and secretively escape. MEANING

EXAMPLE

After stealing my peanut butter he decided to decamp into the night, only to come back 30 minutes later to steal my jelly.

SIMILAR

flee, disappear, run away

OPPOSITE

stay, remain

(adjective)
LUGUBRIOUS

MEANING

Being sad or mournful.

EXAMPLE

Charlie's lugubrious facial expression let us know that he was in a bad place after the loss of his pet cricket "Gary Green".

SIMILAR

unhappy, gloomy, melancholy

OPPOSITE

happy, joyous, cheerful

ACCISMUS
(noun)

Pretending to not want something when you actually do. MEANING

EXAMPLE

Belinda's accismus showed when she pretended not to like wearing gorilla suits when we saw her wearing one when she drove by.

SIMILAR

coyness, modesty, shyness

OPPOSITE

assertiveness, aggressiveness

(verb)
PREVARICATE

To not tell the whole truth in order to deceive. MEANING

EXAMPLE

Paul's only choice was to prevaricate by blaming the dog when asked by his wife if he peed on the toilet seat.

SIMILAR

beat around the bush, lie

OPPOSITE

be direct, tell the truth

(noun)
ZEUGMA

The use of one word in a sentence that has two different meanings. MEANING

EXAMPLE

An example of zeugma is "When Nate got divorced he lost his house and his mind.".

SIMILAR

figure of speech, trope

OPPOSITE

one word meaning one thing

(adjective)
TIMOROUS

To be nervous or lacking confidence.   MEANING

EXAMPLE

Ryan asked the clerk for the magazine behind the counter in a timorous voice.

SIMILAR

fearful, timid, shy

OPPOSITE

boastful, confident, bold

METANOIA (noun)

A change in thinking usually in a spiritual way. MEANING

EXAMPLE

I experienced a metanoia when the plastic Jesus on my dashboard spoke to me and said "Stop eating cheeseburgers!".

SIMILAR

flip-flop, change of heart

OPPOSITE
sameness, idleness

(noun)
DIALOGIST

A person that is part of a dialog. MEANING

EXAMPLE

I stared at my dialogist waiting for the chance to interrupt the conversation to say I had to go to the bathroom.

SIMILAR

interviewer, talker, speaker

OPPOSITE

listener, spectator

(verb) **APRICATE**

To sunbathe.

MEANING

EXAMPLE

I love to apricate, however, if I stay out longer than five minutes I turn into a lobster.

SIMILAR bask, tan

OPPOSITE

shield, stay indoors

(noun)
CREDULITY

To eager to believe something.

MEANING

EXAMPLE

Ray's credulity really showed when he told me he believed that there's a chemical that turns pee red in a pool.

SIMILAR

gullibility, ignorance, naivety

OPPOSITE

suspicion, distrust

(adjective)

INSOUCIANT

MEANING

To be carefree.

EXAMPLE

The surfer had an insouciant way of thinking about life in that he only needed waves and beef jerky to survive.

SIMILAR

calm, relaxed, chill, untroubled

OPPOSITE

concerned, anxious, hyper

(adjective)

CREPUSCULAR

1. Active or appearing during twilight hours.
2. Having a dark look.

MEANING

EXAMPLE

If you thought vampires were crepuscular creatures, you would be wrong, they are nocturnal.

SIMILAR

dim, foggy, blurry

OPPOSITE

bright, illuminated

(verb)
BEHOOVE

To be necessary or in your best interest. MEANING

EXAMPLE

It would behoove you to learn how to fly a plane before jumping in the cockpit and winging it.

SIMILAR

to be advisable, be suitable

OPPOSITE

discourage, fail, refuse

(verb)
ASSUAGE

To ease the burden of something. MEANING

EXAMPLE

Lucy tried to assuage her feelings of guilt for eating the kids' sausages by offering them some loose change from her purse.

SIMILAR

relieve, calm, lessen

OPPOSITE

make difficult, aggravate

(noun)

CURMUDGEON

MEANING

A old grumpy person.

EXAMPLE

The old curmudgeon living down the street always yells obscenities at me when I tell him to wear clothes when he cuts his lawn.

SIMILAR

grump, an agitated person

OPPOSITE

a friendly old person

(noun)

DIPHTHONG

A sound made by putting two vowels together in one syllable. MEANING

EXAMPLE

"ou" is a diphthong used to spell "house" and Americans and Canadians pronounce this word differently.

SIMILAR

semivowel, plosive

OPPOSITE

hiatus, one vowel syllable

USURP (verb)

MEANING
To take by force.

EXAMPLE

Jay tried to usurp my position as leader of The Noisy Nerds band but it didn't happen because he sucks at singing.

SIMILAR

steal, take over, seize

OPPOSITE

give back, surrender

VELLEITY

(noun)

A small desire to do something. MEANING

EXAMPLE

He has the velleity to be a hand model but it probably won't happen because his fingernails are really gnarly.

SIMILAR

impulse, inclination, leaning

OPPOSITE

dislike, hatred

PERFIDIOUS

(adjective)

Being deceitful or disloyal.

MEANING

EXAMPLE

The perfidious son took his father's riding lawnmower and sold it to feed his ice cream addiction while his father was on vacation.

SIMILAR

unfaithful, dishonest, two-faced

OPPOSITE

faithful, honest, one-faced

(adjective)
LOQUACIOUS

MEANING

Tending to talk too much.

EXAMPLE

Holly becomes so loquacious when talking about shoe shopping you would think her jaw would fall off.

SIMILAR

talkative, chatty, wordy

OPPOSITE

silent, quiet, reserved

(adjective) **ADROIT**

Skillful with the hands
and/or mind. MEANING

EXAMPLE

Although he might not think so
himself, Rivers is an adroit
guitar player when it comes to
solos.

SIMILAR

handy, gifted, polished, clever

OPPOSITE

clumsy, amateurish, maladroit

INUNDATE (verb)

1. To overwhelm.
2. To flood.

MEANING

EXAMPLE

The fast-food employee was so inundated with orders, that she quit right there, jumped out of the drive-thru window, and ran away.

SIMILAR

overload, overpower

OPPOSITE

underwhelm, empty

(adjective)

COMPENDIOUS

MEANING

Short but to the point.

EXAMPLE

This ebook is a compendious compilation of how to crossbreed a snail with a Beretta Pigeon, to which the offspring is known as a "Snail Gun".

SIMILAR

short and sweet, concise

OPPOSITE

rambling, long-winded

(noun)

SUBTERFUGE

A tricky action to get what you want. MEANING

EXAMPLE

Jessica felt she needed to use subterfuge to trick the double agent into giving up his shoe phone.

SIMILAR

cheating, deception, tactic

OPPOSITE
openness, honesty

(noun)

RECIDIVISM

The act of committing a crime again after being punished. MEANING

EXAMPLE

The **dim-witted** politician said the rate of recidivism would go down if convicts were given their own lemonade stands upon their release from prison.

SIMILAR

relapse, backslide, reoffending

OPPOSITE

improvement, betterment

(adjective)

SAGACIOUS

Able to make good judgments.

MEANING

EXAMPLE

Only a sagacious art collector would know that a digital image of an ape would now be worth millions of dollars.

SIMILAR

perceptive, smart, clever

OPPOSITE

dumb, moronic, stupid

(noun)
TEMERITY

MEANING

Excessive boldness.

EXAMPLE

I was surprised at Tyler's temerity when he asked for a bigger discount on the antique toilet seat when it was already 90% off.

SIMILAR

audacity, forwardness

OPPOSITE shy, reserved,

(noun)
MISANTHROPE

A person who hates other people. MEANING

EXAMPLE

It was confirmed that the old man was a misanthrope when he sold everything except his jigsaw puzzles and moved to the woods.

SIMILAR

grump, skeptic, loner

OPPOSITE
human lover, people person

(adjective)

DOGMATIC

Being sure that your ideas are the only rights ones.

MEANING

EXAMPLE

He was very dogmatic in his stance that insect cruelty was wrong, that he wouldn't even harm the cockroach that crawled into his ear.

SIMILAR

opinionated, arrogant

OPPOSITE
open-minded, flexible

(verb)

CONFABULATE

To chat informally.

EXAMPLE

It was hard to understand Rhonda when she would confabulate about lip injections because her lips were too big.

SIMILAR

to chitchat, shoot the breeze

OPPOSITE

be silent, not speaking

(noun)

CATHARSIS

The process of releasing emotions in order to feel relief. MEANING

EXAMPLE

Hearing the song "You Don't Need A Girl Who Likes Muscle Men" was a great catharsis for me after losing my girlfriend to a professional wrestler.

SIMILAR

freeing, cleansing, ridding

OPPOSITE

repressing, keeping, hiding

(adjective)
PERSPICACIOUS

Having accurate judgment
or understanding. MEANING

EXAMPLE

The perspicacious wife knew her
husband was cheating on her
the moment she smelled on him
that nasty perfume her sister
wears.

SIMILAR

perceptive, sharp, observant

OPPOSITE

stupid, unattentive, slow

(adjective)

IGnominious

MEANING

Causing shame.

EXAMPLE

Amy's loss in the cake contest was an ignominious failure due to the fact she used salt instead of sugar to make her cake.

SIMILAR

embarrassing, shameful

OPPOSITE

glorious, honorable

(verb)

AMELIORATE

MEANING

To improve something.

EXAMPLE

Dan tried to ameliorate the problem of the gum stuck in Lily's hair by applying peanut butter and mayonnaise.

SIMILAR

enhance, fix, amend

OPPOSITE

worsen, leave alone

(adjective)

LACHRYMOSE

Being on the verge of tears.

A lachrymose expression started to appear on little Timmy's face when the bully stole his pet rock.

tearful, weepy

cheerful, happy, joyful

PERIPATETIC

(adjective) Being nomadic.

(noun) A traveler.

MEANING

EXAMPLE

The peripatetic nature of the rockstars job allowed him to collect snow globes from every city he visited.

SIMILAR

wandering, traveling, roving

OPPOSITE

domesticated, settled

(adjective)

OBSEQUIOUS

MEANING

Very eager to obey.

EXAMPLE

Bob was such an obsequious team member that when the coach asked him to wash the player's socks and underwear by hand, he would do it with a smile on his face.

SIMILAR

submissive, brown nosing

OPPOSITE

domineering, arrogant

(adjective)
STENTORIAN

MEANING

Being really loud.

EXAMPLE

The teacher's stentorian voice shook me to the core when he yelled "What do you want to do with your life?".

SIMILAR
booming, roaring, powerful

OPPOSITE
quiet, silent, soft

(adjective)

INEFFABLE

Too great to be described in words.

MEANING

EXAMPLE

The man felt ineffable happiness as he gazed at the double rainbow.

SIMILAR

astonishing, undescribable

OPPOSITE

believable, imaginable

(noun)

SYBARITE

A person who likes luxury
and pleasure.

MEANING

EXAMPLE

Jack was considered a sybarite
for his habit of eating caviar
while taking a dump on his
gold-plated toilet.

SIMILAR

libertine, hedonist

OPPOSITE

saint, purist

(adjective)
PROPITIOUS

Something that is
favorable. MEANING

EXAMPLE

The timing couldn't have been
more propitious for the
starving family to come across
a fluffle of rabbits.

SIMILAR

favorable, promising, lucky

OPPOSITE

unlucky, unfortunate

(adjective)

MYOPIC

1. Not able to see things far away.   MEANING
2. Not understanding.

EXAMPLE

Louis fell out of favor with the crafts club for his myopic stance on glue-gun control.

SIMILAR

nearsighted, narrow minded

OPPOSITE

farsighted, insight

(adjective)

DeSULTORY

Showing little interest or effort. MEANING

EXAMPLE

Uncle Roofus's desultory effort to put together my bike lead to the front wheel falling off and me with a broken wrist.

SIMILAR

halfhearted, casual, random

OPPOSITE

focused, systematic

(adjective)

INVIDIOUS

Tending to cause MEANING
discomfort or resentment.

EXAMPLE

I was put in an invidious
position when asked by the bully
if I would rather drink from the
toilet or lick the urinal puck.

SIMILAR

awkward, difficult, unpleasant

OPPOSITE

desirable, pleasant

(adjective)

SERAPHIC

To be angelic or innocent.

Do not be fooled by the child's seraphic appearance, he put gasoline in my aftershave bottle and aftershave in my gas tank.

holy, heavenly, divine

evil, demonic, wicked

(noun)

APPARITION

MEANING

A ghost.

EXAMPLE

As Brent slowly opened his eyes he noticed the apparition of his dead guinea pig "Carlos" floating above his head.

SIMILAR

spirit, specter, phantom

OPPOSITE

a living person or thing

BONHOMIE (noun)

Kindness and/or friendliness. MEANING

EXAMPLE

My father is mostly known for his bonhomie except for before he has his morning coffee, that's when he is a grump.

SIMILAR
warmth, happiness

OPPOSITE

coldness, meanness, cruelty

(adjective)

PROSAIC

Lacking creativity or boring. MEANING

EXAMPLE

He was perfectly content every morning with his prosaic breakfast of plain white toast and water.

SIMILAR

bland, unimaginative, dull

OPPOSITE

creative, cool, inspiring

SOBRIQUET (noun)

MEANING

A nickname.

EXAMPLE

After Luke threw up during the spelling bee his sobriquet became "Pukie Lukie".

SIMILAR

moniker, handle

OPPOSITE

real name, birth name

(noun) # TORPOR

The state of being inactive physically or mentally.

MEANING

EXAMPLE

She was so tired and hungry that when she got home she devoured a box of donuts and fell into a deep torpor.

SIMILAR

inactivity, slowness, laziness

OPPOSITE

energy, vigor, strength

(adjective)

DISCURSIVE

Randomly moving from one topic to the next. MEANING

EXAMPLE

The anatomy professor's discursive lecture on the inner workings of the spleen left half the class confused and the other half asleep.

SIMILAR

rambling, meandering, wordy

OPPOSITE

concise, to the point

(adjective)

QUOTIDIAN

MEANING

Happening on a daily basis.

EXAMPLE

My grandparent's quotidian schedule consists of waking up, eating walnuts, watching game shows, then going to bed.

SIMILAR

everyday, usually, uninteresting

OPPOSITE

unusual, exciting, spontaneous

(noun)
RACONTEUR

MEANING

A skillful story teller.

EXAMPLE

It takes quite the raconteur to come up with a story about a boy with magic powers that goes off to a magic school.

SIMILAR

narrator, orator, tale spinner

OPPOSITE

listener, audience, spectator

(adjective)
WIZENED

To be wrinkled due to age.

MEANING

EXAMPLE

All those years living in Florida turned Gloria into a leathery and wizened prune of a woman.

SIMILAR

withered, worn, shrunken

OPPOSITE

taut, tight, fresh

FETID (adjective)

MEANING

Smelling really bad.

EXAMPLE

Funky Fumes from Fred's fetid feet were the result of a fungus from a frog farm.

SIMILAR

stinky, foul, smelly

OPPOSITE

fragrant, pleasant smelling

(adjective)

DILATORY

To be slow leading to delay.

MEANING

EXAMPLE

The author's dilatory pace of writing the book caused his publisher a lot of anxiety, which lead to a nervous breakdown.

SIMILAR

sluggish, lax, lazy, slothful

OPPOSITE

fast, prompt, on time

(adjective)

VERDANT

To be green with grass or plants.

MEANING

EXAMPLE

My neighbor used to have a verdant lawn but he lost his job and had to let the gardener go so now it looks like crap.

SIMILAR

grassy, leafy, lush

OPPOSITE

parched, dry, waterless

(noun)

VENDETTA

1. A lingering grudge.
2. A blood feud.

MEANING

EXAMPLE

Angela has had a personal vendetta against me ever since I dropped a worm in her hair in grade school.

SIMILAR

dispute, conflict, vengeance

OPPOSITE

truce, cease-fire, agreement

(adjective)

DISGRUNTLED

To be annoyed or
dissatisfied.

MEANING

EXAMPLE

The disgruntled postal worker
quit the post office and now
works in the fashion industry
where there is less stress.

SIMILAR

angry, resentful, irked

OPPOSITE

contented, happy, satisfied

(adjective)

CAPACIOUS

Being spacious and able to hold a large quantity.

MEANING

EXAMPLE

He must have a capacious stomach to hold six hot dogs, a pound of anchovies, a hot fudge sundae, and a jar of mayonnaise without puking.

SIMILAR

roomy, sizeable, big

OPPOSITE

cramped, small, tiny

(noun)
PRIVATION

The state of being deprived of what is needed to exist. MEANING

EXAMPLE

The hillbillies lived a life of privation until one day when Uncle Jed found oil on their land, now they live in Beverly Hills.

SIMILAR

poverty, suffering, misery

OPPOSITE

luxury, lavishness, rich

(noun)

VARIeGATeD

Having different colors, marks, or patterns.

The man's variegated hairstyle led the woman to believe he was a degenerate punk rocker when in fact he was a physics professor.

multicolored, colorful

one color, plain, monochrome

eXTRICaTe (verb)

To free someone or something from difficulty.

Annie tried to extricate herself from the embarrassing situation of having food stuck in her teeth by quickly rinsing with her champagne.

remove, get out, withdraw

snarl, involve, entangle

(adjective)

COMMODIOUS

MEANING

Being big and comfortable.

EXAMPLE

Upon moving from Texas to New York City, the cowboy realized he would not find an apartment commodious enough for him and his horse.

SIMILAR

roomy, spacious, grand

OPPOSITE

small, tiny, unconfortable

PARSIMONY

(noun)

The quality of being careful with money.

MEANING

EXAMPLE

Due to my mother's parsimony, my family had to recycle everything including toothpaste and toilet paper.

SIMILAR

frugal, miserliness, cheap

OPPOSITE

generous, giving, charitable

UNDULATE

(verb)
To move up and down.

(adjective)
Having a wavy apperance.

Grant's hips were undulating to the disco music with such velocity that every girl on the dance floor was mesmerized.

going up and down, side to side

motionless, static, stopped

(verb)

DEPRECATE

To express strong
disapproval.   MEANING

EXAMPLE

The bishop would deprecate the
priest for getting a tattoo of
the Virgin Mary.

SIMILAR

bad-mouth, despise, critize

OPPOSITE

praise, honor, celebrate

(adjective)

ANTIQUATED

Being old-fashioned and out of date.

MEANING

EXAMPLE

My basement has such an antiquated look with fake wood paneling, shag carpet, and bean bag chairs with duct tape holding the beans in.

SIMILAR

ancient, behind the times

OPPOSITE

fresh, new, modern

(verb)

PEREGRINATE

MEANING

To walk from place to place.

EXAMPLE

Barry decided to peregrinate from Boston to L.A. but only made it as far as Brookline.

SIMILAR

travel, roam, journey

OPPOSITE

be stationary, not moving

(adjective)

FASTIDIOUS

Caring about detail and wanting everything to be perfect. MEANING

EXAMPLE

The fastidious restaurant owner fired the millennial server for texting on her phone even though there were no customers.

SIMILAR

meticulous, critical, fussy

OPPOSITE

messy, sloppy, not picky

(noun)

LASSITUDE

A lack of energy in mind and body.

MEANING

EXAMPLE

After Thanksgiving dinner, Burt experienced a lassitude when the tryptophan from the turkey kicked in.

SIMILAR

tiredness, fatigue, sleepiness

OPPOSITE

energy, vigor

(adjective) TURGID

1. To be arrogant with words. *MEANING*
2. To be swollen.

EXAMPLE

Sean tried to mansplain how the algorithm worked to Nancy, but it came out sounding turgid so Nancy just walked away.

SIMILAR

congested, overblown, pompous

OPPOSITE

modest, simple, plain

BANAL (adjective)

To be boring and absent of creativity.

MEANING

EXAMPLE

Being stuck in a broken-down elevator for an hour with a chatty woman and banal music playing on the speaker would drive any person crazy.

SIMILAR

common, overdone, predictable

OPPOSITE

creative, fresh, new

(noun)

INDIGNATION

The anger felt after something unjust was done. MEANING

EXAMPLE

Chris felt such indignation when Chad pulled his bathing suit down in front of Elaine, especially because he just had gotten out of the pool.

SIMILAR

resentment, upset, distress

OPPOSITE

happiness, contentment

(adjective)

FURTIVE

MEANING

Being done in a secretive way not to be found out.

EXAMPLE

Jake's furtive affair with the boss was finally exposed when Ron, from accounting, caught them kissing in the broom closet.

SIMILAR

sneaky, sly, hidden

OPPOSITE

open, exposed, displayed

AUGURY

(noun)

A prediction of something
coming in the future.

MEANING

EXAMPLE

The best augury pertaining to
living in a metaverse could be
that plastic surgery may
become a thing of the past.

SIMILAR

omen, prophecy

OPPOSITE

hindsight, observation

(adjective)
LEXICAL

Relating to words.

Because of Ken's lexical shortcomings, he was unable to answer most of the SAT questions.

linguistic, verbal

nonlinguistic, nonverbal

(adjective)

CONTRITE

Feeling guilty for something.

EXAMPLE

When I walked into the room I found my son looking very contrite standing against the once white wall now covered in marker.

SIMILAR

sorry, regretful, ashamed

OPPOSITE

defiant, unrepentful

ALOOF (adjective)

MEANING

Being antisocial.

EXAMPLE

Marilyn is an aloof teenager who always wears black and carries a pet rat named "Dark Lord" around in her backpack.

SIMILAR

cool, distant, unfriendly

OPPOSITE

warm, outgoing, friendly

(noun) enmity

MEANING
A feeling of hate toward someone or something.

EXAMPLE

John received nothing but enmity when the girl's basketball team found out he was really a man mid-season.

SIMILAR

dislike, ill will, hostility

OPPOSITE

goodwill, friendship, like

PROPAGATE

(verb)

To spread out and multiply.

MEANING

EXAMPLE

The aliens from planet Zobsnad would soon propagate their species around planet Earth and make the humans their pets.

SIMILAR

breed, spread, grow

OPPOSITE

deplete, lessen, destroy

(adjective)
unctuous

1. Someone over the top with flattery. MEANING
2. Greasy texture.

EXAMPLE

The unctuous used car salesman convinced me to buy a fluorescent green sedan with a crushed orange velvet interior.

SIMILAR

cringy, oily, creepy

OPPOSITE

blunt, to the point

PEDANT (noun)

MEANING

A person who shows off how smart they are.

EXAMPLE

The pedant in the backseat of my car, also known as Earl, better stop telling me how to drive or he's walking back to the trailer.

SIMILAR

academic, pompous intellectual

OPPOSITE

anti-intellectual

(adjective)
FELICITOUS

1. Being a good match.
2. Pleasing. MEANING

EXAMPLE

Scott is rather dumb, so playing a rock in the school play is a felicitous part for him.

SIMILAR

fitting, suitable, favorable

OPPOSITE

inappropriate, disagreeable

(adjective)
VACUOUS

MEANING

1. To be stupid.
2. To be empty.

EXAMPLE

The girl's speech was full of vacuous points about the proper way to clip a dog's nails.

SIMILAR

dull-witted, vacant, mindless

OPPOSITE

intelligent, meaningful

(adjective)

SOMNOLENT

Having the effect of sleepiness. MEANING

EXAMPLE

With the lecture about the spiny snail combined with the professor's somnolent voice, most of the students were asleep within ten minutes.

SIMILAR

tired, drowsy, boring

OPPOSITE

wide awake, alert, energized

(adjective)

INDEFATIGABLE

MEANING

Unable to get tired out.

EXAMPLE

Joe's indefatigable spirit keeps him going even though he hates his job as a septic tank cleaner.

SIMILAR

persistent, relentless

OPPOSITE

feeble, weak, tired

MALAPROPISM (noun)

The misuse of words with similar sounds.   MEANING

EXAMPLE

The class laughed at Britney's malapropism on career day when she said she wanted to be an inferior designer.

SIMILAR

slip of the tongue

OPPOSITE
correct word usage

(noun)
xenophobe

A person who fears or
hates strangers or
foreigners. MEANING

EXAMPLE

The president of the chess club
was accused of being a
xenophobe because he wouldn't
let any of the exchange
students join.

SIMILAR

prejudice person, bigot

OPPOSITE

open-minded, liberal

(adjective) TERSE

Using only a few words in
an unfriendly way. MEANING

EXAMPLE

My father replied with a terse
"Get a job!" when I asked him
for 10 bucks.

SIMILAR

abrupt, blunt, brief

OPPOSITE

long-winded, polite

(noun)

POLYMATH

A person with a lot of knowledge in many subjects.

MEANING

EXAMPLE

My team "Beer Bros" never wins on the pub's trivia night because we are always beat by team "Nerd Rangers" who are a bunch of polymaths.

SIMILAR

scholarly, educated, academic

OPPOSITE

ignorant, uneducated

(noun)

EFFLUVIUM

MEANING

A bad smell coming from waste or decaying matter.

EXAMPLE

After eating a pot of chili, my brother proceeded to the bathroom where he produced such a nasty effluvium that the paint started peeling off the walls.

SIMILAR

stinky fumes, odor, exhaust

OPPOSITE

nice aroma, pleasing fragrance

HUBRIS (noun)

Extreme pride and arrogance.

MEANING

EXAMPLE

Isaac had so much hubris when talking about how great he was at cooking he didn't notice his quiche was burning behind him.

SIMILAR

self-importance, conceit

OPPOSITE

modesty, humbleness

(adjective)

GAUCHE

Lacking grace and being socially awkward.

MEANING

EXAMPLE

It was a bit gauche when Pastor Dan farted in church during his sermon, but it was also funny.

SIMILAR

uncultured, graceless

OPPOSITE

cultured, graceful

(adjective)

OPPROBRIOUS

Expressing strong criticism.

MEANING

EXAMPLE

His opprobrious remarks about my job as a professional clown made me cry and that ruined my makeup.

SIMILAR

insulting, scornful, offensive

OPPOSITE

approving, complimentary

(adjective)

DIMINUTIVE

Being very small.

MEANING

EXAMPLE

When Santa made fun of the elf's diminutive stature, he was so upset that he quit making toys and became a dentist.

SIMILAR

little, petite, tiny, short

OPPOSITE

big, enormous, tall

(verb)

JeTTISON

To throw away something
that is not needed or a
burden. MEANING

EXAMPLE

Because of the bad snow storm,
Santa was forced to jettison
half the Christmas presents
from his sleigh.

SIMILAR

get rid of, dump, toss

OPPOSITE

keep, save, hold on to

(adjective)
TAWDRY

Having a cheap or shoddy appearance.   MEANING

EXAMPLE
Our neighbor's tawdry Christmas tree was decorated with ornaments made from beer cans and fishing lures, and a used paper plate with a star drawn on it at the top.

SIMILAR
flashy, tasteless, trashy

OPPOSITE
refined, elegant, posh

(noun)
CONTRETEMPS

1. A small argument.
2. An accidental
occurrence.   MEANING

EXAMPLE

There are always contretemps
between members of my family
during Christmas over who has
the ugliest sweater.

SIMILAR

squabble, disagreement, mishap

OPPOSITE
agreement, help

(noun)
ECCHYMOSIS

Bruises made from bleeding under the skin. MEANING

EXAMPLE

My grandmother was treated for ecchymosis after she was run over by a reindeer earlier this evening.

SIMILAR
contusion, spot, mark

OPPOSITE
clear skin, lack of bruises

(adjective)

nonPLUSSeD

MEANING

Being so surprised you don't know what to do.

EXAMPLE

Thinking the last Christmas present was winter boots, you wouldn't believe how nonplussed I was after opening it to find the video game console I wanted.

SIMILAR

bewildered, mystified

OPPOSITE

not bothered, unaffected

(adjective)
seQuenT

Coming one after the
other in order. MEANING

EXAMPLE

For Hanukkah, the eight candles
of the menorah are lit in
sequent order for eight days
with a shamash, also known as
the helper candle.

SIMILAR

consecutive, continuous

OPPOSITE

disorganized, disturbed

(adjective)

DIFFIDENT

To be **shy** and **lack confidence.**

MEANING

EXAMPLE

Although he is usually quite the party animal, he becomes very diffident when there are pretty girls around.

SIMILAR

bashful, introverted, timid

OPPOSITE

outgoing, confident

(noun)

eFFRONTERY

Bold and rude behavior.

MEANING

EXAMPLE

Rob had the effrontery to hit on the man's wife, take a sip of his beer, and eat some of his fries.

SIMILAR

audacity, nerve, gall

OPPOSITE

shyness, timidity, introvert

(adjective)

PETULANT

To be easily angered or annoyed.

MEANING

EXAMPLE

The petulant passenger eventually made the flight crew so angry that they duct-taped him to his seat and put a barf bag in his mouth.

SIMILAR

moody, touchy, impatient

OPPOSITE

easygoing, well-mannered

(noun)
GENTRIFICATION

A process where a poor neighborhood turns into a wealthy one. MEANING

EXAMPLE

Since gentrification started in my neighborhood, I now see dudes with man buns, drinking eight-dollar coffee while walking their teacup dogs on every corner.

SIMILAR

restoration, urban-renewal

OPPOSITE

reverse gentrification

(noun)

SKULDUGGERY

MEANING

Dishonest behavior.

EXAMPLE

It is believed that Dr. Kane got the part on the TV show with the use of skulduggery in the form of bribing the producers with free lip injections and butt lifts.

SIMILAR

funny business, trickery

OPPOSITE

directness, openness, honesty

ABOUT THE AUTHOR

ALBERT B. SQUID

If you spot this person please call our HOTLINE at 867-5309 ask for Tommy.

Born to a family of construction peeps, ALBERT B. SQUID was raised on construction sites in Massachusetts. Believe it or not, he holds two degrees in Engineering and Architecture and has worked as an Architect in Boston, Tokyo, and Seoul. In the year 2000, Squid started an independent children's book publishing company in NYC. I had fun doing that.....I mean HE (Albert B. Squid) had fun doing that! After becoming a freelance voice actor, the elusive author's whereabouts are unknown. He was last seen in the town of Shaike in the East African country of Djibouti learning traditional disco dance. Squid recommends if you go to Shaike, Djibouti get lessons from the dance teacher named K.C.

GET YOUR BIRTHDAY WORD

T-SHIRT

DEC 31

(noun)

SKULDUGGERY

MEANING

Dishonest behavior.

EXAMPLE

It is believed that Dr. Kane got the part on the TV show with the use of skulduggery in the form of bribing the producers with free lip injections and butt lifts.

SIMILAR

funny business, trickery

OPPOSITE

directness, openness, honesty

GET YOUR BIRTHDAY WORD

NFT

DEC 31

(noun)

SKULDUGGERY

MEANING

Dishonest behavior.

EXAMPLE

It is believed that Dr. Kane got the part on the TV show with the use of skulduggery in the form of bribing the producers with free lip injections and butt lifts.

SIMILAR

funny business, trickery

OPPOSITE

directness, openness, honesty

Printed in Dunstable, United Kingdom